21st CENTURY LIVES
TEEN MOVIE STARS

Debbie Foy

WAYLAND

First published in 2009 by Wayland

Copyright © Wayland 2009

Wayland
338 Euston Road
London NW1 3BH

Wayland Australia
Level 17/207 Kent Street
Sydney, NSW 2000

Senior editor: Camilla Lloyd
Designer: Simon Borrough
Picture researcher: Diana Morris

Picture Acknowledgments: The author and publisher would like to thank the following for allowing their pictures to be reproduced in this publication: Cover & 8: Richard Young/Rex Features; Henry Lamb/BEI/Rex Features: 6, Kristin Callahan/Rex Features: 12, Lions Gate/Everett/Rex Features: 11, Matt Barron/BEI/Rex Features: 5, 20, MGM/Everett/Rex Features: 19, Peter Brooker/Rex Features: 9, Rex Features: 17, Rune Hellestad/Corbis: 14, Sipa/Rex Features: 1, 10, 16, 18, Sony Pics/Everett/ Rex Features: 21, Stewart Cook/Rex Features: 4, W. Disney/Everett/Rex Features: 7, Warner Br/ Everett/Rex Features: 13, 15.

British Library Cataloguing in Publication Data:
Foy, Debbie
    Teen movie stars. - (21st century lives)
    1. Motion picture actors and actresses - Biography -
    Juvenile literature
    I. Title
    791.4'3'028'0922

ISBN: 978 0 7502 5691 9

Printed in China

Wayland is a division of Hachette Children's Books, an Hachette UK company

www.hachette.co.uk

Contents

Zac Efron
The Sweet Life of Zac Efron

Zac Efron has been described as 'arguably the biggest star in the USA right now'.

" I grew up in California and was completely ignorant of the entertainment industry. I was a regular guy with a regular life. I went to school and got good grades. I have the most normal family in the world and was always involved with sports. "

Zac Efron, *Chicago Sun Times*, 19 August 2007

Name: Zachary David Alexander Efron

Date and place of birth: 18 October 1987, San Luis Obispo, California, USA

Education: Zac attended Arroyo Grande High School where he achieved good grades and loved playing sports. He graduated in 2006 and was accepted at the University of Southern California but deferred his entry so that he could concentrate on film projects.

Big Break: At the age of 14 Zac auditioned for a little-known Disney project called *High School Musical*. He got lucky and Zac was cast in the male lead role, Troy Bolton.

Famous films: *The Derby Stallion* (2005), *High School Musical* (2006), *High School Musical 2* (2007), *Hairspray* (2007), *High School Musical 3* (2008), *Seventeen Again* (2009), *Me and Orson Welles* (2009).

Acting style: In his career so far Zac has played innocent guys with a squeaky-clean image. He is also the popular choice for musicals with his strong singing and dancing talent.

Top awards: In 2007 Zac was presented with a Young Hollywood Award: One to Watch for his part in *Hairspray*. In 2008 he received an MTV Movie Award for Best Breakthrough Performance.

Star quality: Zac is a true teen heart throb with his sun-streaked hair, blue eyes and wide smile.

Something you may not know about him: Zac has two Australian Shepherd dogs called Dreamer and Puppy, and a Siamese cat named Simon.

Since the release of the *High School Musical* films, Zac Efron's face most likely adorns the bedroom walls of millions of young girls all over the world. The *High School Musical* phenomenon catapulted Zac Efron into the realms of teen superstardom, and with three *High School Musical* films under his belt and plenty of new projects on the go, he looks set to remain a poster boy for teens and 'tweens' (slang term for children between the ages of 9 and 12) for some time to come!

Zac was born to an average middle-class family in California, USA. His parents worked in the local power plant and Zac and his younger brother Dylan attended the nearby high school. His father encouraged Zac's interest in acting and singing and Zac appeared in several theatre productions at school and took piano and singing lessons.

At the age of 14 Zac's drama teacher recommended him to an acting agency in Los Angeles and his early TV appearances included *ER, Summerland* and *The Suite Life of Zack & Cody*. In 2003 he starred in a television movie called *Miracle Run*, playing the part of an autistic twin. For his performance he was nominated for a Young Artist Award for Best Performance in a TV Movie.

In the meantime Zac and his mother were making the six-hour return journey every month to Los Angeles, for Zac to attend castings and try-outs. After many gruelling auditions, including a marathon seven hours of singing and dancing on one occasion, Zac was told he had landed the role of Troy Bolton in the original *High School Musical* movie.

The original *High School Musical* movie went on to produce a mega-hit DVD, the biggest selling CD of 2006 and is regarded as one of the most popular TV movies of all time. Zac's career was launched, and since then he has made two *High School Musical* sequels and was cast as the lead, Link Larkin, in the highly successful film version of *Hairspray*. It has been reported that Zac has signed up to appear alongside Johnny Depp in *Pirates of the Caribbean 4*.

Though Zac has expressed a desire to move away from musical roles and focus instead on more serious acting, it is undeniable that he has sung and danced his way to the top of his profession and into a lot of young girls' hearts!

Zac Efron and Vanessa Hudgens at the High School Musical 3 *press conference in May 2008.*

"I saw this sweet, goofy kid and I thought he was too light. Link Larkin is more cool. Then one of the executive producers said to me, 'You passed on him? Are you out of your mind? He's the biggest star on the planet to anyone under 15.'"

Adam Shankman, director and choreographer, on how he almost didn't cast Zac Efron in the lead role in *Hairspray, USA Today,* 20 July 2007

Lindsay Lohan
Teen Drama Queen

Name: Lindsay Dee Lohan

Date and place of birth: 2 July 1986, New York City, USA

Education: Lindsay attended high school until Year 11 and from that time she was taught at home. She graduated through the famous distance-learning school Laurel Springs High, Ojai, California.

Big Break: A leading role in *The Parent Trap* (1998).

Famous films: *The Parent Trap* (1998), *Freaky Friday* (2003), *Confessions of a Teenage Drama Queen* (2004), *Mean Girls* (2004), *Herbie Fully Loaded* (2005).

Acting style: Lindsay is known for her cute 'teen-next-door' and high school diva roles, but her brand of comedy can be intelligent and heart warming.

Top awards: In 1999 Lindsay received a Young Artist Award for the Best Leading Young Actress in a Feature Film for *The Parent Trap*. In 2005 she received a MTV Movie Award for Best Female Performance in *Mean Girls*.

Star quality: Lindsay has literally grown up on screen and enjoys the Hollywood scene. In recent years the media have been obsessed with Lindsay Lohan's transformation from cute kid to stylish woman.

Something you might not know about her: Lindsay was the first red-haired child ever to be signed by the prestigious Ford Modelling Agency.

Lindsay Lohan supports several charities and is pictured at this event in Madison Square Garden, New York in September 2008.

66 **It's something different to experience, it's something I've always aspired to do and have, and I love it. I think it's so cool - they want my picture!** 99

Lindsay Lohan on fame and celebrity, www.bbc.co.uk/films

One of the early movies that shot Lindsay to stardom was Freaky Friday.

Lindsay Lohan rose to fame as Hollywood's teen movie queen. By the age of 17 she had played lead roles in four major films and under the glare of the Hollywood media spotlight, the world has watched Miss Lohan transform from sweet kid to budding style icon. Her face has rarely been out of the press either. The media report on her every movement, from her successes to her rumoured celebrity 'burn out' as a result of over-work or too much partying!

Lindsay Lohan's career began at the tender age of three when she began modelling and appearing in TV advertisements for companies such as The Gap and Pizza Hut. At the age of ten she made her acting debut in a long-running television drama called *Another World*, and not long after, Lindsay was hand-picked to star in her first feature film – a Disney production called *The Parent Trap*. In the film she played the roles of twin sisters and her success led to Disney signing her up for a three-movie contract.

After a brief break in which Lindsay launched her singing career she returned to the Disney film set to make the 2003 box office hit *Freaky Friday*. In 2004 she released her successful first music album *Speak* and also starred in the comedy movie *Confessions of a Teenage Drama Queen*. Though it was never a major hit, film critics were impressed by Lindsay's portrayal of the wannabe actress, Lola.

Mean Girls (2004) was Lindsay's first non-Disney film and proved to be another box office success, confirming her status as the ultimate teen movie queen. She returned to Disney in 2005 to star in *Herbie: Fully Loaded*, with the intention that her new 'non-high school' role would allow her to make the transition into more grown-up films.

Though she has made at least one film a year since *Herbie: Fully Loaded*, none have reached the box office heights of her 'teen' movies. However, Lindsay Lohan continues to attract intense media interest and her personal and family relationships, feuds with fellow starlets, health issues and career low-points have all been portrayed in newspapers and magazines across the world. Let's hope she can escape the glare of the media spotlight to allow her talent to shine through in her up-and-coming movies.

"She's so natural at what she does. I've never seen one take where she's off. The difference between her and the other girls that are naughty in the business is that she's actually talented."

Lati Grobman, film producer, *People* magazine, 16 June 2008

Daniel Radcliffe & Emma Watson

The Darlings of Hogwarts

Daniel and Emma attend the Empire Film Awards in London 2006 to accept the Outstanding Contibution Award for the work done on the Harry Potter films released so far.

> **"I like being challenged. Even when you're doing really intense, dramatic scenes that take so much out of you it's still really fun and energizing. Acting makes you feel so alive."**
>
> **Daniel Radcliffe, *The Guardian*, 11 October 2006**

Name: Daniel Jacob Radcliffe; Emma Charlotte Duerre Watson

Dates and places of birth: Daniel: 23 July 1989, London, England; Emma: 15 April 1990, Paris, France

Education: Daniel attended City of London, an all-boys private school. Emma went to private schools in Oxfordshire and achieved As in all her GCSEs and A-Levels.

Big Break: Both actors had their big break when they were cast in the roles of Harry Potter and Hermione Granger in the first *Harry Potter* film.

Famous films: Daniel and Emma have starred in *Harry Potter and the Philosopher's Stone, Harry Potter and the Chamber of Secrets, Harry Potter and the Prisoner of Azkaban, Harry Potter and the Goblet of Fire, Harry Potter and the Order of the Phoenix* and *Harry Potter and the Half-Blood Prince* (2001–2009).

Acting styles: Most of Daniel's career to date has been playing the boy wizard, but he is expanding his talents into more serious roles. Emma is known for being precise and rarely has to re-take her scenes.

Top awards: In 2006 Emma won an award for Best Female Performance and in 2007 Daniel won an award for Best Male Performance, both at the ITV National Movie Awards.

Star quality: Emma loves hanging out with her friends and insists on being treated like an ordinary teenager. It was Daniel's 'charm and simplicity' that caught the eye of the casting agents and producers.

Something you may not know about them: In July 2007 Daniel and Emma, along with cast member Rupert Grint, who plays Ron Weasley, left their hand, foot and wand prints in the concrete outside the famous Grauman's Chinese Theatre in Hollywood (see picture on page 9).

In 2000 the search was on to find a young actor who could bring to life the character of a boy wizard, playing the lead role in *Harry Potter and the Philosopher's Stone* - the first screen adaptation of J. K. Rowling's highly successful novels. The *Harry Potter* films count as probably the literary world's most successful phenomenon and the expert casting of Daniel Radcliffe and Emma Watson played an enormous part in this success.

Daniel Radcliffe is the only child of Alan Radcliffe and Marcia Gresham, and he grew up in London. For a bit of fun at the age of ten he auditioned for his first acting role and was cast as the young David Copperfield in a TV adaptation of the Dickens' play.

Daniel, Emma and Rupert make their wand prints.

When first approached to audition for *Harry Potter* his parents turned it down, but after a chance meeting with the producer David Heyman in a theatre audience one night, Daniel's parents were persuaded to allow their son to audition for the boy wizard role. Daniel was elated to discover that he had won the role and fliming of the *The Philosopher's Stone* began in September 2000. The film was released in November 2001 and went on to become the second highest earning film ever made after *Titanic*.

Daniel found himself on the covers of entertainment magazines and had hundreds of TV appearances in the UK and USA. The bespectacled boy wizard with the lightning scar on his forehead developed an enormous fan following, and in Daniel Radcliffe, a star was born.

When the author of the *Harry Potter* books, J. K. Rowling chatted to Emma Watson (Hermione Granger) on the phone after her casting she was immediately struck by just how perfect she thought Emma was for the role. Emma was born in Paris and moved to Oxford with her mother where she grew up with her younger brother. Emma was cast as Hermione at the age of nine having only acted previously in school plays. She was put forward for the *Harry Potter* auditions by her school drama teacher and the casting agents were impressed by her confidence, maturity and composure.

Emma has made a name for herself as a mature and accomplished actor starring alongside Daniel in the five *Harry Potter* films screened to date, but both young actors hope to spread their wings beyond Hogwarts! Daniel has appeared in *December Boys* (2007), a film set in Australia and in a West End play called *Equus* in which he plays a young stable boy who is obsessed with horses.

But Potter fans have no fear! Daniel and Emma are scheduled to appear in *Harry Potter and the Half Blood Prince* due for release in 2009. *Harry Potter and the Deathly Hallows (parts I and II)* are planned for 2010 and 2011, so look out for more fantastic storylines and stunning special effects as Harry, Hermione, Ron and the gang continue to bring their wicked wizard action to screens near you!

"It was like being reunited with my long lost son. Having seen Daniel's screen test, I don't think Chris Columbus could have found a better Harry."

J. K. Rowling, author of the *Harry Potter* books, www.danradcliffe.co.uk

Scarlett Johansson
Scarlett Fever

Scarlett attends an event at the Metropolitan Museum of Art, New York, May 2008.

> **"I'm not a 'poor me' kind of person. Certain cards were dealt to me, and I had to be strong. My parents divorced when I was 13. The actual separation wasn't hard, but things that come with divorce are difficult. But those things mould you to be the person that you are. I've always been very determined, ever since I was a little girl, to make my way."**
>
> **Interview with Scarlett Johansson, http://www.parade.com, 11 March 2007**

Name: Scarlett Johansson

Date and place of birth: 22 November 1984, New York City, USA

Education: Scarlett attended the Professional Children's School in Manhattan, New York City until she graduated in 2002 at the age of 18. While she was working on films she was tutored on the film set.

Big Break: Though she had appeared in five movies before, it was her performances in *The Horse Whisperer* (1998) and *Ghost World* (2001) that earned her widespread praise and attention.

Famous films: *The Horse Whisperer* (1998), *Ghost World* (2001), *Lost in Translation* (2003), *Girl With a Pearl Earring* (2003), *The Nanny Diaries* (2007), *The Other Boleyn Girl* (2008).

Acting style: Scarlett has a presence on screen that is quite compelling. She often plays thoughtful, intelligent characters.

Top awards: Scarlett won a BAFTA film award for her performance in *Lost in Translation* in 2004 and received a BAFTA nomination for *Girl With a Pearl Earring*. She has also been nominated for four Golden Globe awards for *Girl With a Pearl Earring* (2003), *Lost in Translation* (2003), *Love Song for Bobby Long* (2004) and *Match Point* (2005).

Star quality: Scarlett is known for being mature, super-confident and very alluring.

Something you may not know about her: She has a twin brother, Hunter, who is also an actor. Hunter was born three minutes after Scarlett.

Scarlett Johansson is unlike many Hollywood starlets of her generation. She is not showy or flashy, nor does she seek the limelight. She often plays quiet, thoughtful characters and has the ability to communicate a great deal on screen without words or over-emotional outbursts. Her intense screen presence has resulted in her winning many top awards and she has been nominated for several other awards. What has caused this Scarlett fever?

Born and brought up in New York City, Scarlett loved to sing and dance from an early age. Her mother took her along to several TV commercial auditions but was told that her voice was too husky and her 'look' didn't quite fit. The young Scarlett, however, intrigued movie-casting directors, and by the age of ten she had secured a small part in the film *North*.

By the age of 13 she was starring opposite Robert Redford in *The Horse Whisperer*. Her portrayal of the character Grace MacLean, traumatised by a horse riding accident, won her a Young Star Award in 1998. Scarlett's mother became her manager and this movie, alongside her 2001 performance in *Ghost World*, were the films that put Scarlett Johansson on the map.

Her next two film ventures would propel Scarlett from successful actor to Hollywood superstar! In 2003 she starred alongside Colin Firth in *Girl With a Pearl Earring*, playing a 17th century Dutch housemaid who was the artistic 'muse' of the famous Dutch painter Johannes Vermeer. Her haunting and emotional portrayal of Griet earned her Golden Globe and BAFTA nominations. In the same year she was awarded a BAFTA for her starring role in Sofia Coppola's *Lost in Translation*, the story of a young woman staying in Tokyo who embarks on an unusual friendship with a middle-aged actor.

More recently Scarlett has shown that she also has incredible range and flexibility. She has lent her voice to Mindy in *The SpongeBob Squarepants Movie*, played a sultry and alluring woman in Woody Allen's *Match Point* (2005), featured in a romantic comedy called *The Nanny Diaries* (2007) and starred in the period movie *The Other Boleyn Girl* alongside Natalie Portman in 2008. If her future is as bright as her past, we can expect to see a lot more of this ambitious, talented and intriguing young actress.

Scarlett in her role as Griet in Girl With a Pearl Earring *(2003). This picture is a replica of a picture painted by Johannes Vermeer.*

"She makes you feel like she has been around the world. She has a coolness and a subtlety that you would not expect. You feel like she's seen a lot. She can convey an emotion without saying very much at all."

Sofia Coppola, director of *Lost in Translation, The Observer*, 28 December 2003

Hilary Duff
Disney Princess

Hilary supports various charities and offers her financial support to certain causes. She is pictured here at an event to raise awareness of skin cancer, May 2008.

"I want to be married and have kids, definitely, but not any time soon. A lot of things in my life have come faster than they do for most people."

Hilary Duff, *USA Today*, 2 April 2007

Name: Hilary Erhard Duff

Date and place of birth: 28 September 1987, Houston, Texas, USA

Education: Hilary was mainly home-schooled or was tutored while filming.

Big Break: Hilary's breakthrough from minor TV and extras roles came in 2001 when she began playing the role of Lizzie McGuire in the Disney Channel series of the same name.

Famous films: *Agent Cody Banks* (2002), *The Lizzie McGuire Movie* (2003), *Cheaper by the Dozen* (2003), *A Cinderella Story* (2003), *Cheaper by the Dozen 2* (2005), *Material Girls* (2006).

Acting style: Hilary's acting style suits comedies and light-hearted acting roles.

Top awards: In 2003 Hilary was awarded Teenager of the Year by *Rolling Stone* magazine in the USA. In the same year she received a Young Artist Award for Best Young Ensemble for her role in *Cheaper by the Dozen*.

Star quality: She is used to being in the spotlight and handling the media. She has a professional approach to her work and unlike some of her contemporaries she is never photographed falling out of a nightclub!

Something you may not know about her: Hilary supports Kids with a Cause, a charitable organisation that helps needy children around the world. Last year she donated $250,000 (£125,000) to help the victims of Hurricane Katrina in the USA.

Though now in her 20s Hilary Duff was known as the hardest-working teen star in Hollywood. Her meteoric rise to fame meant that by the age of 18 Hilary had achieved more than many celebrities do in their lifetime. She has made hit movies, recorded several best-selling albums, launched a multi-million dollar clothing line, and is even expanding the Duff brand into perfumes and cosmetics.

Born to an ordinary Texan family, Hilary and her elder sister Haylie were encouraged by their mother to take acting and singing lessons. Eventually they relocated to California with their mother to pursue their dreams, while their father remained in Texas looking after the family's convenience store business. After many auditions the Duff sisters found work in television advertisements and other minor TV roles.

After almost giving up the idea of acting, Hilary auditioned for the children's television series *Lizzie McGuire* where she played the title role of the hapless, average middle school girl and her less than smooth journey into teenhood. In 2001 the Disney Channel's *Lizzie McGuire* shot Hilary to stardom almost overnight, as millions of girls between the ages of 7 and 14 tuned in to watch her.

In 2003 Hilary did not renew her contract with the Disney Channel and was cast in her first major film role as Natalie Connors in *Agent Cody Banks*. In the same year she starred in *The Lizzie McGuire Movie*, which proved to be a worldwide box office success and Hilary began to get her name known as the best young actress for light comedies. Late in 2003 she starred alongside Steve Martin in *Cheaper by the Dozen*, her most commercially successful movie to date. *A Cinderella Story* (2004) saw Hilary playing the modern-day Cinderella, Sam Montgomery, and this she

Hilary and Chad Michael Murray in the modern-day fairytale, A Cinderella Story.

followed with an appearance in *Cheaper by the Dozen 2* (2005). In 2006 Hilary expanded on her role in Hollywood to become a producer on the film *Material Girls*. The big-screen comedy spoof features Hilary playing alongside her real-life sister Haylie.

Her latest movie *Stay Cool* (2009) with Winona Ryder sees Hilary playing a high school girl who flirts with a visiting author to her school. Hilary has made her fortune from playing 'bubblegum' characters and recording teeny pop albums, but Hilary knows her audience, plays to her strengths, works hard and stays true to the Hilary Duff brand.

"Before I got my TV show, it was such a struggle. I was going on hundreds of auditions and not getting any call backs. My mom prepared us really well for handling rejection and not taking it too seriously and stuff. But I feel very lucky and I feel very blessed."

Hilary on auditioning for parts,
http://movies.about.com/od/acinderellastory, 2003

Freddie Highmore
Star of Fantasy Flicks

Freddie at the premiere for Arthur and the Invisibles *(2006).*

" **I'd read the book, but I hadn't seen the original movie before doing *Charlie and the Chocolate Factory*. I thought it was better to wait until afterwards because I thought I ought to create my Charlie on my own. I think the original film is good, but I think it's better now because Charlie is kept more pure. He doesn't drink a bubbly solution and fly off into the roof.** "

Freddie Highmore about playing Charlie, http://uk.movies.ign.com, 15 July 2005

Name: Alfred Thomas Highmore

Date and place of birth: 14 February 1992, London, England

Education: Freddie is currently studying at Highgate School, north London, but while filming he is tutored on set.

Big Break: Freddie has been acting since the age of seven but it was his award-winning performance in *Finding Neverland* that gave him his big break. In the movie Freddie played the role of Peter Llewelyn-Davies, the boy who inspired the book *Peter Pan* by JM Barrie.

Famous films: *Finding Neverland* (2004), *Charlie and the Chocolate Factory* (2005), *The Spiderwick Chronicles* (2008).

Acting style: Freddie has made his name as one of the world's leading child actors in fantasy films. He has a freshness and vitality on screen that lends itself well to the roles of the children he has played, and he is able to deliver emotionally charged scenes with great maturity.

Top awards: Freddie was presented with Broadcast Film Critics Association Awards for Best Young Actor in *Charlie and the Chocolate Factory* in 2006 and for *Finding Neverland* in 2005. In the same year he was also presented with a Golden Satellite Award for Outstanding New Talent for his role in *Finding Neverland*.

Star quality: Johnny Depp (who was Freddie's co-star in *Finding Neverland*) was so impressed with Freddie's performance that he personally recommended Freddie for the role of Charlie Bucket in *Charlie and the Chocolate Factory*.

Something you may not know about him: Freddie is a keen Arsenal FC fan and is learning to play the guitar.

Freddie (pictured far left) plays Charlie Bucket in Charlie and the Chocolate Factory, with Johnny Depp who plays Willy Wonka (third from the right).

Freddie Highmore, one of the hottest teen movie stars of today, began his acting career at the age of seven, and by the age of twelve he had already built up an impressive movie portfolio. Over the last decade the sweet-faced boy with the big, doleful eyes has served up such powerful performances that his profile has been firmly elevated from cute kid actor to serious film-star-to-be-reckoned-with!

Born to a showbiz family (his father, Edward Highmore, is an actor and his mother is one of the UK's leading theatrical agents) Freddie began to audition for TV parts because he thought it would be a fun thing to do. With no drama training behind him, in 1999 he secured a part in *Women Talking Dirty*, playing alongside the famous actor Helena Bonham Carter. Several TV appearances followed before he was asked to film the movie *Two Brothers* (2004), which follows the life of two tiger cubs. Freddie had an amazing time filming on location in Cambodia.

However, it was his role in *Finding Neverland* (2004) that really launched Freddie's career. Starring alongside Johnny Depp and Kate Winslet, Freddie was praised for his mature and powerful portrayal of Peter Llewelyn Davies, the boy who inspired the book *Peter Pan*. After playing the role of Charlie Bucket in Tim Burton's *Charlie and the Chocolate Factory* (2005), Freddie's reputation as the go-to kid for fantasy films

was cemented and in 2008 he starred in *The Spiderwick Chronicles*, based on the popular children's stories, starring in the dual roles of twins Simon and Jared Grace. Again, he was widely praised – this time for delivering the two roles simultaneously and so adeptly.

Freddie has also lent his voice to several movies, proving his scope and flexibility. In 2007 he voiced the part of Lyra's daemon, Pantalaimon, in *The Golden Compass*, based on the popular book by Phillip Pullman. Other voice-over work for Freddie has included a part-animated, part live-action trilogy of films by Luc Besson entitled *Arthur and the Invisibles* (2006), *Arthur and the Vengeance of Maltazard* (2009) and *Arthur and the War of Two Worlds* (due for release in 2010). Freddie will also be offering his vocal talents once again in 2009 as the voice of Astro Boy in a film of the same name. Fitting for a young guy whose acting talent is out of this world!

"Freddie is quite something else. I would literally get hairs up on the back of my neck watching this kid act."

Kate Winslet, www.backstage.com, 7 January 2005

Christina Ricci
Indie Teen Queen

Christina attends the glamorous Cannes Film Festival in May 2008.

❝I remember when I was little, all the mothers saying once you're 13 you have to stop working because there are no roles for teenagers. But I think I was lucky ... For a while it did look like I would have to keep doing kids' movies to stay in the business, but then *The Ice Storm* came along.❞

Christina on film roles for teenagers, *Interview* magazine, February 2004

Name: Christina Ricci

Date and place of birth: 12 February 1980, Santa Monica, California, USA

Education: Christina attended local elementary and high schools in the New York suburbs of Montclair, New Jersey. After a year of high school she left to attend The Professional Children's School in New York City.

Big Break: Christina's break into movies came when she was cast to play Cher's youngest daughter in *Mermaids* (1990).

Famous films: *The Addams Family* (1991), *Addam's Family Values* (1993), *Casper* (1993), *The Ice Storm* (1997), *Sleepy Hollow* (1999), *Penelope* (2008).

Acting style: She has a strong on-screen charisma and since she began acting has mostly been cast as dark, quirky or unconventional characters.

Top awards: In 1999 she was nominated for a Golden Globe for *The Opposite of Sex*. In 2000 she won a Saturn Award for *Sleepy Hollow*, and in 2001 she was presented with a Young Hollywood Award for The Hottest and Coolest Young Veteran!

Star quality: She is well-known for her glowing pale skin, fabulous spooky look and scrutinising glare!

Something you may not know about her: For her film *Black Snake Moan* (2007) Christina ate nothing but sugary foods to achieve the unhealthy appearance required by her character!

At the age of eight, Christina turned up to an acting audition with a black eye and shocked the casting director! This was a taster of what her acting future would be like as a teenager. Since then Miss Ricci has made great movies playing kooky, unconventional or downright freaky characters, and continues to do so today.

Christina was born and lived in California until the age of three. Her mother was a former model and her father a psychiatrist. The youngest of four children, Christina's urge to perform was revealed in an elementary school play in which she provoked the child playing the lead to punch her!

Christina stars as Katrina Van Tassel in Tim Burton's Sleepy Hollow *(1999).*

Her big screen debut came in 1999 when she was cast in *Mermaids* alongside Cher, Bob Hoskins and Winona Ryder. She was a serious child and so found playing oddly intense and very serious children easy. Christina made enough of an impression in *Mermaids* to secure her more work and the following year she was cast as the ghoulish Wednesday Addams in The *Addams Family* (1991). This movie and its sequel *Addams Family Values* (1993) were huge box office successes and during her teenage years Christina was in huge demand.

In 1995 Christina starred in the comedy ghost movie *Casper* and a 'coming-of-age' movie entitled *Now and Then*, starring as one of four 12-year-old girls and their friendship during the 1970s to 1990s. *The Ice Storm* in 1997 was Christina's first 'grown up' role and at the age of 17 she proved she was able to make the often tough transition from child star to adult actor.

In 1998 she starred as the dangerously manipulative Dedee Truitt in *The Opposite of Sex*. At the age of 19 she won or was nominated for several prestigious awards including a Golden Globe nomination. In the same year she co-starred with Johnny Depp in Tim Burton's fairy tale horror movie *Sleepy Hollow*. Playing Katrina Van Tassel confirmed Christina's title as the queen of independent films.

In her 20s Christina has continued to make popular movies, including *Penelope* in 2007 in which she co-starred with Scottish actor James McAvoy and Reese Witherspoon. Playing an aristocratic girl who had been cursed with a pig's nose, again revealed her desire to play shocking or unconventional roles.

Christina is one of the most successful actors of her generation. With her haunting glare and deadpan delivery she is one of the few child stars to make the transition into adult roles and continue to be a huge box office draw.

"Ricci was an early queen of weird. Perhaps it is the contrast so evident in her features – her sweet, heart-shaped face and her melodic, girlish voice are both offset by her deep brown eyes. Those pools of ambiguity once prompted the *Sleepy Hollow* director Tim Burton to remark that 'when she looks at you, you get a definite feeling, but you're not quite sure what that feeling is'."

Interview with Will Lawrence,
www.entertainment.timesonline.co.uk,
19 January 2008

Thomas Sangster

Hollywood Calling

Thomas Sangster attending the premiere of Nanny McPhee *in Los Angeles, 2006. His co-stars in the movie were Emma Thompson and Colin Firth.*

❝As soon as the clapboard goes or the guy shouts 'action', I immediately switch to another person. I always fit a bit of me into every character I play.❞

Thomas Sangster,
www.dailymail.co.uk/
tvshowbiz/reviews, 5 October 2007

Name: Thomas Brodie Sangster

Date and place of birth: 16 May 1990, London, England

Education: Thomas attended Pimlico School in south London. He has never attended drama school nor had acting lessons. He suffers from a mild form of dyslexia.

Big Break: Though Thomas had appeared in several television films during 2001 and 2002, he won his first major film role with *Love Actually* at the age of 12.

Famous films: *Love Actually* (2003), *Nanny McPhee* (2005), *The Last Legion* (2007), *Tintin* (due for release 2010).

Acting style: Thomas has made his name playing children who are younger than him because he has innocent, boyish looks and is quite small for his age.

Top awards: Thomas has been nominated for six awards including the Young Artist Awards in 2007 and 2008 for Best Young Actor in *Nanny McPhee* and *The Last Legion*, respectively.

Star quality: Likeable and down-to-earth, Thomas enjoys going back to school after filming as he feels his friends 'ground' him and stop him from becoming too star struck!

Something you may not know about him: Thomas is the second cousin of Hugh Grant, who coincidentally, was one of his fellow co-stars in *Love Actually!*

Perhaps you have spotted him in the popular children's movie *Nanny McPhee* or heard his voice as Ferb on the Disney Channel's *Phineas and Ferb*, but it is a fair bet that his upcoming movie projects will make Thomas Sangster a household name over the next few years!

Born into a theatrical family (his parents are both actors), Thomas was bitten by the acting bug while watching his parents perform on stage in Prague, Czech Republic. At the age of ten and with no acting lessons behind him, he began trying out for auditions through his parents' acting agent. After appearances in several television films including *Stig of the Dump*, Thomas was cast in the role of Sam in the successful British film *Love Actually*, appearing alongside Hugh Grant, Colin Firth, Emma Thompson and Kiera Knightly.

In 2005 Thomas appeared alongside Emma Thompson and Colin Firth again in the film *Nanny McPhee*, where Thomas plays Simon Brown, the eldest of seven children. In 2007 Thomas's starring role was a more serious one. He acted alongside Colin Firth (again!) and Sir Ben Kingsley as Romulus Augustus, the child ruler and last Roman emperor in *The Last Legion*. His youthful, elfin kind of look meant that although he was 17 at the time of filming Thomas was actually playing the part of a 12-year-old boy!

Spurred on by his film nominations the promising young actor sent off an audition tape to Hollywood director Stephen Spielberg in the hope of landing a part in Stephen King's *The Talisman* – a project that never actually got off the ground. However, luck was on Thomas's side for when Spielberg saw the tape he realised he had found the boy who could play Tintin, the character created by Belgian cartoonist, Herge.

Thomas playing the role of the boy king, Romulus Augustus in the movie, The Last Legion (2007).

Thomas was signed up for Spielberg's three-movie project to bring the boy reporter to life on the big screen using the latest 3D technology. So keep your eyes peeled for this south London boy – with Hollywood behind him he's sure to go far!

"They had already clocked Thomas for the role before I came on board. I kept my fingers crossed that he would be cast, and when they tested those boys, he won hands down. He's a terrific actor."

Colin Firth on Thomas Sangster's casting in *The Last Legion*, www.dailymail.co.uk/tvshowbiz/reviews, 5 October 2007

Kirsten Dunst
Spider-Man's Girl

Kirsten was winner of the Female Star of the Year 2007 at the ShoWest Award Ceremony in Las Vegas, USA.

Name: Kirsten Caroline Dunst

Date and place of birth: 30 April 1982, New Jersey, USA

Education: She attended the Ranney School in New Jersey until sixth grade (age 11) then moved to California. She graduated from Notre Dame High School, a private Catholic high school in Sherman Oaks, Los Angeles, in 2000.

Big Break: Her breakthrough film was *Interview with a Vampire* (1994) in which she played vampire Claudia, alongside Tom Cruise and Brad Pitt.

Famous films: *Interview with a Vampire* (1994), *Jumanji* (1995), *The Virgin Suicides* (1999), *Bring It On* (2000), *Spider-Man* (2002), *Spider-Man 2* (2004), *Tangled Web: The Love Triangles of Spider-Man 3* (2007), *How to Lose Friends and Alienate People* (2008).

Acting style: She often plays highly likeable characters. Her on-screen chemistry with Tobey Maguire, the actor who played Spider-Man, was credited with adding the 'romantic soul' to the *Spider-Man* movies.

Top awards: In 1995 Kirsten was nominated for a Golden Globe for her role in *Interview with a Vampire*, and also won an MTV award for the same movie. She won an Empire Award and an MTV Award for Best Actress in *Spider-Man* (2003).

Star quality: What amazes people about Kirsten is her ability to carry roles in teen romances or action blockbusters, then switch to deeper, darker, off-beat roles in independent films.

Something you may not know about her: Her name is pronounced 'Keer-sten' not 'Kur-sten' as many people think!

❝ **Dunst is one of the very few child actors to have made an irrefutably triumphant transition from child actor to grown-up star.** ❞

Interview with Hadley Freeman, guardian.co.uk, 26 April 2007

Kirsten (Mary-Jane Watson) and Tobey Maguire (Peter Parker/ Spider-Man) in a scene from Spider-Man 3 (2007).

By the age of six Kirsten Dunst was already on her way to becoming a movie star. She had been modelling and shooting TV commercials from the age of three and at six years old she made her acting debut. Small roles in feature films followed, including an appearance in Woody Allen's *New York Stories*. All the early signs showed she had great potential, so in 1992 Kirsten, her mother and brother moved to Los Angeles to pursue her career.

Fortunately for Kirsten, she did not have the years of struggle that can often plague the life of a young Hollywood hopeful. She worked consistently in TV until 1994 when Kirsten was catapulted to stardom via her role in *Interview with a Vampire*. Though she was only 11 years old, Kirsten's mature portrayal of Claudia, who is both girl and woman, earned her wide praise and a Golden Globe nomination. In 1995 she followed up her success by co-starring with Robin Williams and a whole host of computer-generated animals in the box office hit, *Jumanji*.

Throughout her teens, Kirsten began to stand out from the young Hollywood hopefuls with her consistently excellent performances in films such as *The Virgin Suicides* (1999), directed by Sofia Coppola, and box office hit *Bring It On* (2000). But it was casting her in the role of Mary Jane Watson in *Spider-Man* that sent Kirsten's career stratospheric, and overnight she became hot property!

The on-screen chemistry between Kirsten and Tobey Maguire was widely commented on as film critics felt that it was the charm of their up-and-down relationship and Kirsten's likeability as the sweet Mary-Jane Watson that gave *Spider-Man* its 'soul'. Two more *Spider-Man* movies followed in which Kirsten alternated these crowd-pleasing box office hits with quieter, more serious films such as *Eternal Sunshine of the Spotless Mind* (2004) and *Marie Antoinette* (2006) in which she played the leading role.

With rumours of several hit movies in the pipeline it looks like Kirsten Dunst won't be retiring from the big screen any time soon. If she continues to evolve as an actress, displaying her great range and versatility, expect to see this talented child-turned-teen-turned grown-up actor on a screen near you!

"I attended a normal school and worked on movies in vacations. If a film overlapped with school time, I took my school work with me."

Kirsten Dunst on her experiences as a teenaged movie star, www.timesonline.co.uk, 4 July 2004

Other Teen Movie Stars

The Olsen Twins

Mary-Kate and Ashley Fuller Olsen were born on 13 June 1986 in Los Angeles, California, USA. At the age of nine months, both twins played the same role of Michelle Tanner on the show *Full House*. The show ran for eight years and the Olsens became two of the most popular characters on television.

The girls' parents and managers created Dualstar Entertainment, a company that would manage the twins' public image and organise the selling of Olsen twins' dolls, books and other products. Merchandising of their image has become a multi-million dollar empire. Around the same time the girls made several direct-to-video movies including *To Grandmother's House We Go* (1992) and *How the West Was Fun* (1994). In 1995 *It Takes Two*, their first big-screen film, was released. It was hugely successful when released on video. Ashley and Mary-Kate have continued to make films including *Passport to Paris* (1999), *When in Rome* (2002) and *New York Minute* (2004). Mary-Kate's first acting appearance without Ashley was in the movie *Factory Girl* in 2006, starring Sienna Miller.

The Olsen 'brand' has started to develop fashion interests with successful clothing lines. The twins are now also popular TV presenters. More movies are likely to be on the way, but, as the twins get older, their careers may take an exciting new turn. Stay tuned...!

Macaulay Culkin

Macaulay Carson Culkin was born on 26 August 1980 in New York City, USA. The third child of seven, his mother was a telephone operator and his father worked in the local Catholic church.

Macauley began acting at the age of four appearing in TV and film productions in the 1980s. At the age of nine he was cast in the comedy movie *Uncle Buck* but it was his role as Kevin McCallister in *Home Alone* (1990) that started Macaulay Culkin on his path to fame. The movie *My Girl* followed in 1991, but it was the blockbuster sequel *Home Alone 2: Lost in New York*, that confirmed Macaulay's status as the most successful child performer since Shirley Temple in the 1930s and '40s. As a result of his prolific movie appearances he became the highest paid child actor ever.

His films of the early nineties: *The Good Son* (1993), *Getting Even With Dad* (1994), and *Richie Rich* (1994) were disappointments at the box office. In 1994 at the age of 14 Macaulay suddenly dropped out of acting. At 23 he made a comeback with *Party Monster* (2003) and *Saved!* (2004). Though neither film was a great success they helped to restart his career and recently he has started to do voice-over work.

Natalie Portman

Natalie Portman was born Natalie Hershlag on 9 June 1981 in Jerusalem, Israel. She is an only child and her father is Israeli and her mother American. When Natalie was three years old the family moved from Israel to Washington DC, USA.

At the age of four Natalie began dancing lessons and at ten, she turned down a modelling contract to pursue her acting. An excellent student, she attended Jewish elementary and high schools, and later graduated from Harvard University with a pshychology degree.

In 1994 she won the part of Mathilda in Luc Besson's film *Leon*. Soon after she got the role she adopted her grandmother's name and began to use 'Natalie Portman' as her stage name. In the mid-1990s, she appeared in a slew of acclaimed, big-budget movies, including *Heat* (1995) starring Robert De Niro and Al Pacino, *Mars Attacks!* (1996) with Jack Nicholson and Glenn Close and *Beautiful Girls* (1996) with Matt Dillon.

In the late 1990s Natalie was cast as Padme Amidala in the *Star Wars trilogy*. The first movie in the trilogy, *Star Wars Episode 1: The Phantom Menace* opened in 1999 and catapulted Natalie into the limelight. While filming the *Star Wars trilogy* Natalie was also studying at university and during her summer break in 2000 she filmed *Star Wars Episode II: Attack of the Clones*. Natalie then starred alongside Julia Roberts in *Closer* in 2004. The final *Star Wars* prequel *Star Wars Episode III: Revenge of the Sith* was released worldwide in May 2005. In 2008, Natalie was in the successful period film *The Other Boleyn Girl* with Scarlett Johansson.

Jamie Bell

Jamie Bell was born on 14 March 1986 in Billingham, England, where he grew up with his mother and older sister, Cathryn. Jamie attended Stagecoach Theatre School and was a member of the National Youth Music Theatre. His grandmother, mother, aunt and sister were all dancers and while waiting outside the door of his sister's dance practices he imitated the dancers inside. At the age of six, his family encouraged him to join the dance school.

In 1999 he successfully beat over 2,000 boys for the title role of *Billy Elliot* (2000). Jamie's life story has similarities with Billy in that he kept his dancing a secret from his friends at school for fear that they would tease him; in the movie Billy Elliot tries to keep his dancing secret from his working class father who disapproves. Jamie's thoughtful and entertaining performance in his film debut earned him a BAFTA Award for Best Actor in 2001.

After *Billy Elliot* Jamie took the part of Smike

in an all-star cast version of *Nicholas Nickleby* (2002) and *Deathwatch* (2002), a horror film set in World War I. In 2005 he was cast in the blockbuster movie *King Kong* (2005). He appeared as the title role in *Hallam Foe* (2007) and he was in *Jumper* (2008). Jamie Bell has avoided the stereotyping trap that many young actors fall into. The sheer range and diversity of his films are a testament to his enormous talent.

Drew Barrymore

Drew Blyth Barrymore was born on 22 February 1975 in California, USA. She hails from a long line of American actors and the director Stephen Spielberg is her godfather.

She began acting at the age of 11 months when she appeared in a TV advertisement for dog food. In 1982 when she was just seven years old she appeared as the precocious Gertie in the science fiction blockbuster movie *E.T. The Extra-Terrestrial*. She quickly became one of Hollywood's most recognised actresses and was expected to behave in a way far beyond her years. Perhaps as a result of the pressure on her, Drew had a troubled childhood and was sent to a special rehabilitation centre to help her overcome her problems.

During her much-publicised childhood she appeared in a handful of films, including *Irreconcilable Differences* (1984) for which she received a Golden Globe nomination, and *Babes in Toyland* (1986). Drew's star continued to rise during her late teens with acclaimed performances in *Poison Ivy* (1992), *Bad Girls* (1994) and *Batman Forever* (1995).

Since leaving her teens Drew has started up a production company Flower Films, and was cast in hit movies such as *Scream* (1996), *The Wedding Singer* (1998), *Charlie's Angels* (2000) and *Donnie Darko* (2001). Her recent movies to watch out for are *He's Just Not That Into You* (2008) featuring Scarlett Johannson and Ben Affleck, and *Everybody's Fine* (2009) co-starring Robert De Niro. Barrymore is back!

Index

21st Century Lives

Contents of more books in the series:

British Olympians
978 0 7502 5946 0
Rebecca Romero
Ben Ainslie
Rebecca Adlington
Lee Pearson
Sarah Storey
Chris Hoy
Eleanor Simmonds
Tim Brabants
Christine Ohuruogu
Other British Olympians

Radio DJs
978 0 7502 5688 9
Chris Evans
Chris Moyles
Christian O'Connell
Jo Whiley
John Peel
Johnny Vaughan
Nihal
Sara Cox
Zane Lowe
Other Radio DJs

Reality TV Stars
978 0 7502 5690 2
Jordan
Leona Lewis
Ben Fogle
Cheryl Cole
Kelly Osbourne
Will Young
Myleene Klass
Lee Mead
Kerry Katona
Other Reality TV Stars

Soap Stars
978 0 7502 5689 6
Ada Nicodemou
Jack P. Shepherd
Kara Tointon
Kym Valentine
Lacey Turner
Roxanne Pallett
Patsy Palmer
Scott Maslen
Samia Smith
Other Soap Stars

Teen Movie Stars
978 0 7502 5691 9
Zac Efron
Lindsay Lohan
Daniel Radcliffe & Emma Watson
Scarlet Johansson
Hilary Duff
Freddie Highmore
Christina Ricci
Thomas Sangster
Kirsten Dunst
Other Teen Movie Stars

WAYLAND